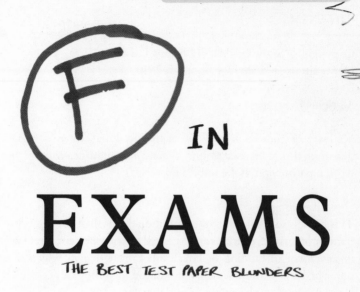

(F) IN

EXAMS

THE BEST TEST PAPER BLUNDERS

Richard Benson

F IN EXAMS

Summersdale Publishers Ltd
46 West Street
Chichester
West Sussex
PO19 1RP
UK

www.summersdale.com

Printed and bound in China

ISBN: 978-1-84953-100-9

Contents

Introduction

Remember those nail-biting times when you were up until the early hours cramming your head with facts and equations that you would never encounter in the real world? Did you wake up the next morning only to find sheets of paper stuck to your forehead but your brain empty of any useful information? In the eerie silence of the school hall you sat staring at the ominous white paper in front of you and the only fact you could recall was your name. Sound familiar? If so, you'll be relieved to discover that you are not the only person on this planet to have experienced such agony.

This book is full to the brim with funny examples of creative answers from clueless but canny students. And in a society where you get higher marks for 'F**k!' rather than a simple 'f**k', you can't really blame them for trying. With a nostalgic nod to your inner teenager you will find yourself chortling through Chemistry, giggling at Geography and ha-ha-ing at History.

Thank goodness school's out for you!

Subject: **Chemistry**

What is a nitrate?

It is much cheaper than a day rate.

Give a brief explanation of the meaning of the term 'hard water'.

Ice

What is a vacuum?

Something my Mum says I should use more often.

What is the process for separating a mixture of chalk and sand?

It is a process called flirtation

What is the process where steam turns into water?

Conversation

What is methane?

Methane is a smelly greenhouse gas which is produced when trees and/or cows are burned.

What is the meaning of the term 'activation energy'?

It's what is needed to get up in the morning.

In a blast furnace it is impossible for aluminium to be extracted from its ores. Why?

Because it is bloomin' hot!

It was predicted in 1988 that tin reserves would only last until the year 2006. However, 18 years later, there are still enough reserves to meet industry demand. Why is this?

Because people are not buying so many tins of baked beans.

Over the last 50 years there has been a significant change in the concentration of carbon dioxide. Give a reason for this.

It's easily distracted.

What are the characteristics of crude oil?

Coarse and rude

Describe the chemical differences between H_2O and CO_2.

H_2O is hot water,
CO_2 is cold water

What is a vibration?

There are good vibrations and bad vibrations. Good vibrations were discovered in the 1960s

The burning of fossil fuels which contain carbon produces a gas called carbon dioxide. Draw a 'dot-and-cross' diagram to represent carbon dioxide.

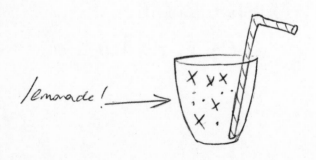

lemonade!

Suggest two reasons why it is important for people to be able to detect food colour additives.

1. To make sure it's in date
2. To arrange it nicely on the plate

Open-cast mining of copper ore creates an extremely large hole. Identify one problem that open-cast mining of copper causes to the environment.

If you don't look where you are going you can fall in the hole.

Calcium carbonate breaks down when heated to over 1500°C. Write an equation to show what takes place.

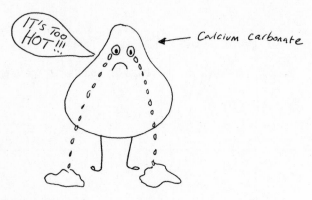

IT'S TOO HOT !!!

← Calcium carbonate

Identify two benefits of using instrumental methods of analysis.

1. Kids always enjoy a subject more when music is involved.

2. I can practise my drumming in science.

Subject: Biology

What is the lowest frequency noise that a human can register?

A mouse

What is the highest frequency noise that a human can register?

Mariah Carey.

Adam cuts his arm. Blood gushes out and is red in colour.

What does this show?

He is not a robot,
he's a real boy!

What is a fibula?

A little lie

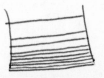

What is the meaning of the word 'varicose'?

Close by

What does 'terminal illness' mean?

when you become ill at the airport.

Biology

State a type of fungus and explain one of its characteristic features.

The Bogey Man. He is green.

What happens when your body starts to age?

When you get old your organs work less effectively and you can go intercontinental.

What happens during puberty to a boy?

He says goodbye to his childhood and enters adultery.

Give an example of a smoking-related disease.

Early death

Biology

What are the three different types of blood vessels?

Vanes, anchovies and caterpillars.

Karen goes into her garden one morning and finds the leaves covered in a sticky substance. What is this substance?

When the leaves sit in the sunshine they get hot and it makes them sweat.

What is a plasmid?

A high definition television

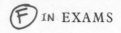

How is oxygen loaded, transported and unloaded in the bloodstream?

By forklift truck

Biology

Explain the concept of homeostasis.

It is when you stay at home all day and don't go out.

In the Hawaiian Islands there are around 500 different species of fruit fly. Give a reason for this.

There are approximately 500 varieties of fruit

Explain the word 'Genome'.

It is an abbreviation of the two words:

Gender and Gnome.

Draw a diagram to represent the human body and label the positions of all the major organs including: brain, heart, lungs and kidneys.

Biology

Draw a diagram indicating the location of the appendix.

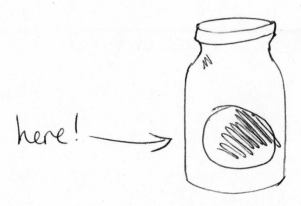

here! ⟶

Below is a diagram of the heart. Please label the relevant sections.

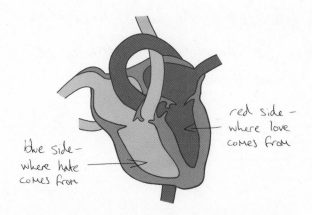

blue side — where hate comes from

red side — where love comes from

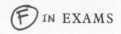

What is a cadaver?

It is a make of a car

What is a fossil?

A fossil is the remains of an extinct animal. The older the fossil, the more extinct the animal is.

What happens to your body when taking a breath?

Your chest gets bigger.

What is the world's largest living mammal?

The woolly mammoth

31

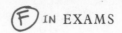

Explain what the theory of evolution states.

My sister used to be a monkey

Identify one form of medicine used to kill bacteria in the body.

Domestos

Biology

Describe one potential consequence of the greenhouse effect on the environment.

All the animals and peoples turn green.

What does 'biodiversity' mean?

A wide range of washing powder.

Sometimes plants have to compete with other plants in order to survive. Suggest two things plants might compete for.

1. Lady Plants
2. Miracle Grow

Subject: **Physics**

Steve is driving his car. He is travelling at 60 feet/second and the speed limit is 40 mph. Is Steve speeding?

He could find out by checking his speedometer.

Explain the word 'momentum'.

A brief moment

Physics

What was Sir Isaac Newton famous for?

He invented gravity.

Is the moon or the sun more important?

The moon gives us light at night
when we need it. The sun only provides
light in the day when we don't.
Therefore the moon is more important.

Currently, the Sun is in a stable period.
State two balanced forces in the Sun

Page 3 and the footie pages

When a star's life cycle is over there is a possibility it will become a black hole. Describe a 'black hole'.

Something very dark in the ground and it looks like this

Many people don't like eating radiation treated food. How could a food scientist prove that radiation treated food is safe?

By eating some!

Name an environmental side effect of burning fossil fuels.

Fire

Describe what happened during the 'big bang'.

A lot of noise.

Why would living close to a mobile phone mast cause ill health?

You might walk into it.

Physics

Give the names of two gases that might contribute to global warming.

1. Bottom gas
2. Cow burps

Hannah sprays her new bike purple. The spraying of the bike gives it a negative charge and the paint a positive one. Why is this?

Positive – spraying is easier than using a paintbrush.

Negative – purple isn't a good colour for a bike.

What is the National Grid?

It is a very large free barbecue in public parks.

What does the National Grid do?

Cooks Sausages to perfection.

What does a transformer do?

It can go from being a robot to a dragster in three seconds.

Give an example of a step-up transformer.

An exercise machine

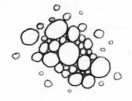

Give a reason why people would want to live near power lines.

You get your electricity faster.

Give three ways to reduce heat loss in your home.

1. Thermal underwear

2. Move to Hawaii

3. Close the door

Physics

Mobile phones are very popular. Give one advantage and one disadvantage of owning a mobile phone.

Advantage You can order a takeaway for your school lunch.

Disadvantage Your parents can get hold of you at any time.

What instrument do you use to measure temperature?

A trambone.

It is possible to generate electricity using energy from the wind. Wind-powered generators do not produce carbon dioxide. Why is this?

They are too busy generating electricity

List three types of electromagnetic wave.

1. Tidal wave
2. Shock wave
3. Mexican wave

What is the name of the theory which suggests that the universe began from a very small point?

The year dot theory.

What is our galaxy called?

Galaxy Caramel

How does the moon remain in a virtually circular orbit around the earth?

God Only Knows

Subject: **Geography**

RM
4
TS

Explain the dispersal of various farming types in Britain.

The cows + pigs are distributed in different fields so they don't eat each other

Explain what is meant by the term 'pastoral farming'.

It's a farm run by vicars.

Define the phrase 'commercial farming'.

It is when a farmer advertises his farm on T.V to get more customers.

Define the phrase 'subsistence farming'.

It's when a farmer doesn't get any assistance

Define the term 'intensive farming'.

It is when a farmer never has a day off.

State three drawbacks of hedgerow removal.

1. All the cows will escape.

2. The cars drive into the fields.

3. There is nowhere to hide.

What scale do seismologists use to measure the force of earthquakes?

A very strong one (not glass).

Volcanoes occur on what kind of plate margins?

Hot plates.

What happens at the edge of a destructive plate margin?

It breaks!

'Powerful aftershocks rocked the city, fires burned out of control, streets were full of debris and ruined buildings. At least 30 people were injured.'
Which type of natural disaster is being described in the report?

The end of Big Brother

Geography

Name the area of calm at the centre of a storm?

The pie in the sky.

What does the word 'lava' mean?

A pre-pubescent caterpillar

THIS WAY UP

Explain the meaning of the word 'magma'.

Japanese cartoons.

What is lahar?

A city in Pakistan

Geography

Explain the word 'migration'.

Migration is a bad headache.

What is meant by 'a pull factor'?

A big red sports car.

What do we call a person forced to leave their home, perhaps by a natural disaster or war, without having another home to go to?

Homeless ☺

Define the term 'shanty town'.

It is a place where people like beer with lemonade in it.

Define the phrase 'heavy industry'.

An industry that sells tons.

There are many footloose enterprises on an industrial estate.
Define the term 'footloose'.

It means stockings that don't have any feet at the end of them

What was the main industry in Persia?

Cats

The race of people known as Malays come from which country?

Malaria

Name the smaller rivers which run into the Nile.

The Juveniles.

Name six animals which live specifically in the Arctic.

Two polar bears
~~Three~~ Four seals

Inhabitants of Moscow are called ...

Mosquitoes

Name one of the primary products of the Hawaiian Islands.

Grass skirts and flower necklaces

What is the collective name given to the inhabitants of the Philippine islands?

The Philistines

Name one famous Greek landmark.

The most famous Greek landmark is the Apocalypse

What is the name of the highest peak of the Alps?

The highest mountain is Blanc Marge.

Which artificial waterway runs between the Mediterranean and Red seas?

The Savage Canal.

Geography

Name one measure which can be put into place to avoid river flooding in times of extensive rainfall (e.g. in Mississippi).

Flooding in areas such as the mississippi may be avoided by placing a number of big dames into the river

Name one technique used by farmers to improve crop yield.

Farmers mostly increase crops by irritating the land.

Name two animals native to Siberia.

The lynx and the larynx.

What are the Pyramids?

The Pyramids are a large
mountain range which splits
France and Spain

How high is Mount Everest?

Depends how much snowfall it has had since it was last measured.

The Narmada and the Tapi river valleys are said to be old rift valleys. What is a rift valley?

Valleys that have fallen out after an argument.

Suggest three natural causes of flooding.

1. Leaving the tap running
2. A huge fat person jumping in the pool and making all the water splash out.
3. If a baby wets themself

Explain what a food chain is. Give an example with your answer.

A chain of sausages

e.g.

← sausages

How do coastal defences work?

They hide behind big rocks and jump out on the enemy and fight them off the beach.

Identify two characteristics of a tropical storm such as Hurricane Katrina.

Angry and a bit moody ~~Moo~~ because it's a girl storm.

What is meant by the term 'green tourism'?

It means when tourists go round in those big green ponchos because they forgot to pack an umbrella.

2 + 2 = 5

Subject: **Maths**

Change 7/8 to a decimal.

7.8

Name a regular triangle.

a three - sided triangle.

Maths

Find the angles marked with letters.

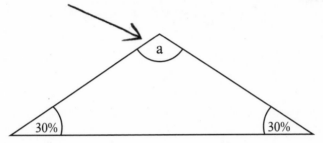

THIS IS THE ANGLE MARKED WITH A LETTER

a

30%   30%

Write two hundred thousand in figures.

two hundred thousand in figures.

What is a six-sided polygon known as?

an empty cage

There are 300 students in Year 10. Mary and Mark want to find out Year 10's favourite colour.

Mary asks 30 people.

Mark asks 150 people.

Mark says 'My conclusions are more likely to be reliable than Mary's'.

Why does Mark think he is right?

Because Mark is a man

A car company is having a sale. A car that was £25,000 before the sale now has 50 per cent off. What is the new price?

Still too expensive.

Expand $2(x + y)$

$2(x+y)$
$2(x + y)$
$2(x + y)$
$2(x + y)$

Simplify the following equation.

$$\sqrt{\frac{5}{5}}$$

$$\frac{\sqrt{5}}{5} = \sqrt{}$$

x is inversely proportional to the square of y.

x=3 and y=4

Express x in terms of y.

$$\cdot -x + \cdot -y = \cdot -)$$

Maths

What is conditional probability?

Maybe, maybe not

What is the splitting formula?

boy meets girl → boy meets another girl
→ girl finds out about other girl
= the splitting formula.
This is not to be confused with the spitting
formula, that's just antisocial.

What is a random variable?

Someone with multiple personalities

What is a discrete random variable?
Give an example with your answer.

It is a person that hides in the corner at parties.
similar to the wall flower but a bit more unpredictable after after a few drinks.

Maths

You are at a friend's party. Six cupcakes are distributed among nine plates, and there is no more than one cake per plate. What is the probability of receiving a plate with a cake on it?

Nil, if my sister is invited too.

What is the symbol for Pi?

← Pi!

John and Julie are both strong badminton players. Is it more probable that Julie will beat John in four games out of seven or five games out of nine?

She will win every game.
She is a girl - girls are
better at these things.

How should Julie play to minimise any loss?

Dirty!

Maths

Calculate a formula for winning the lottery.

buy a ticket -> watch the lottery programme -> turn over to Ant and Dec while the boring bit is on -> turn back to find out that you have missed the important bit -> get cross -> ask your parents what the numbers were -> they are mysteriously absent from the house and return three weeks later after jetting off round the world after cashing in your winnings

On Sunday the ratio of the time Andrew is sleeping to the time he is awake is 3:5. He is sleeping for less time than he is awake. Calculate the number of hours that he is sleeping on Sunday.

Depends what time he sets his alarm for

Write down a number that is less than 184 but larger than 175.

175   42 184

Maths

Write down the number 17,412 to the nearest 100.

$$100 \xleftarrow[near]{} 17,412 \xrightarrow[far]{} 100$$

The sweets in a large jar are shared equally between 20 children. They are given 11 sweets each. How many sweets would each child be given if there were only 12 children?

Not enough sweets

Subject: **Business Studies**

Business Studies

How do the following companies fund themselves?

a) BBC   phone-in competitions

b) ITV   Same as the above

Explain the phrase 'free press'.

When your mum irons trousers for you.

Explain the word 'wholesaler'.

Someone who sells you whole items, e.g. a whole cake.

Assess Fashion House plc's choice to locate its factory near Birmingham. Is Birmingham the right location for this type of business?

No. People from Birmingham aren't very fashionable.

Paul frequently uses the Internet to research information. Suggest two items of information Paul could locate on the Internet which might help him in running his business.

Item 1: www. how-to-run-a-business. com

Item 2: www. how-not-to-run-a-business. com

Suggest three steps Paul is likely to take when selecting the best candidate for a job.

Step one: You're hired

Step two: You're fired

Step three: You're hired

Describe the term 'stakeholder'.

A vampire hunter.
Buffy being the most famous

Hugo King is an engineer. He is a sole trader.
Explain the business term 'sole trader'.

It means he has sold his sole
to the devil!

What is a 'partnership'?

A ship that takes two people to drive

John's net pay is £150. His deductions are £38.

a) Work out John's gross pay.

The money he spends on porn magazines every week.

b) State one mandatory deduction from John's pay.

Beer

c) State one voluntary deduction John may or may not pay.

Tax

Claire used good body language at a job interview.
Can you think of three examples of good body language
that Claire may have used.

1 pole dancing

2 The moonwalk

3 The Bolero

Claire was well prepared for her interview.
Explain how Claire may have prepared herself for the
interview.

Had a bath and put on her
lucky pants.

Business Studies

What does 'quality control' mean?

Those tights mummy wears to make her look thinner.

Suggest two reasons why businesses often want to expand.

1. They want to get bigger to destroy other businesses
2. So they can eat more pies

What does 'limited liability' mean?

It means you aren't very reliable.

Describe an ethical business.

An ethical business is where all the staff are foreign.

Identify two reasons why people can be made redundant from a job.

1. It's cheaper to get someone who isn't so crap.
2. Sleeping with the boss.

Subject: **Psychology**

I think, therefore...

Describe what is meant by 'forgetting'.

I can't remember

Explain a religious theory for the existence of the world.

The big bang was God dropping something

Outline with two examples what is meant by 'unanswered prayers'.

1 Not winning The Lottery

2 Arsenal never winning the league

Freud stated that the superego contains the moral aspect of one's personality. Define the term 'superego'.

A really fast sports car

Psychology

Explain the 'psycho-dynamic approach'.

Using your mind to move things like a jedi

Suggest a way to abate aggression.

If your hands are tied behind your back you can't punch people

Explain the process of 'learning'.

A process by which information goes into one ear and out of the other.

Express the term 'stereotype'.

It is what kind of CD player you own.

Psychology

What does the phrase 'case study' mean?

It is a process whereby you sit and stare at your suitcase before you go on holiday but not knowing what to pack.

Using your knowledge of Freud, provide an example of when a dream represents Freud's theory.

If you dream about biscuits it means you are subconsiously thinking about sex, but if you are dreaming about sex, it means you are thinking about <u>biscuits</u>.

Who said 'I think, therefore I am'?

Please fill in the sections of Maslow's Hierarchy of Needs below.

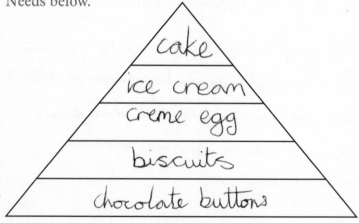

Psychology

Name one factor that influences perception.

Wheva u wear a jonny or not.

Describe one common example of a visual illusion.

Leprechauns

Give one advantage of carrying out surveys.

Opportunity to meet people in the street.

Give one disadvantage of carrying out surveys.

You have to stand out in the cold
for ages with a klipboard

What does the term 'altruism' mean?

No lying.

Explain one common example of the audience effect.

I-max 3-D

Subject: ......**History**......

History

What was introduced in the Children's Charter of 1908?

Children

Name Labour's first cabinet minister.

Mr Chippendale

Where was the American Declaration of Independence signed?

At the bottom.

Name Britain's highest award for bravery.

Probably Nelson's Column

Upon ascending the throne the first thing Queen Elizabeth II did was to…

sit down

What was Sir Walter Raleigh famous for?

He is a noted figure in history because he invented cigarettes and started a craze for Bicycles.

Summarise the key developments of the Industrial Revolution.

Industry revolved

How did Christopher Columbus discover America?

While he was cursing about the Atlantic

Name one of Abraham Lincoln's greatest achievements?

Having his face carved in rock

Summarise the major events of the Cold War.

It started off by someone throwing an ice cream + then someone threw a lolly back.

What were the consequences of the Cold War?

Everyone got really hot what with all that running, fighting in the Snow with Snowballs and riding horses pulling Sledges. No wonder Father Christmas has rosy red cheeks.

Why was the Berlin Wall built?

Germany was competing with China.

Who were the Bolsheviks?

People led by linen

Explain the word 'autocracy'.

A country that has lots of cars.

Explain what is meant by the word 'dictator'.

Someone who reads out loud

Why did Britons have better health after the year 1990?

Because the eighties were over

What was the largest threat to world peace in the 1980s?

Heavy metal, because it was very loud.

Explain what happened during the Night of the Long Knives.

People all over Germany planted their knives in the garden at 7pm and the next morning they had all grown to ridiculous lengths.

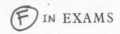

What did Mahatma Gandhi and Genghis Khan have in common?

Unusual names

What does The Statue of Liberty represent?

A green lady holding up a large glass of wine She is wearing a crown. She is the Queen of America.

Name two of the classes which existed in Medieval England.

History class &
Geography class

Identify two methods used to try to prevent the bubonic plague from spreading in 1665.

1. eating marmite — stops things from biting you
2. A catch it, kill it, bin it, campaign

What was the Weimar constitution?

It was a German sausage factory.

What factors enabled Britain to develop a national railway network by 1851?

The invention of trains.

The Nazi party had incredible success in the elections between September 1930 and December 1932. Suggest two reasons for this.

Lots of people voted for them,
Not many people didn't vote for them.

Discuss the significance of the White Rose Movement.

It raised the standards of Chinese resturants throughout the U.K.

Subject: General Studies

Redundancy is often an unpleasant and unexpected event in someone's life. Give two examples of unexpected life events.

1 death

2 rincarnation

Fred has many friends. They all enjoy playing football and drinking in the pub. Fred drinks over 40 units of alcohol each week but the recommended limit is 28. Explain how Fred may be affected by:

a) playing five-a-side football

If he drinks before football he is unlikely to score (goals or girls)

b) drinking 40 units of alcohol each week

He doesn't have much money left at the end of the month

Sally has recently been promoted at work and she received a pay rise. Sally decides to get a credit card for non-essential spending. Can you think of three examples of non-essential purchases Sally may use her credit card for?

1 toilet roll

2 marmite flavoured crisps

3 Gucci handbag

Employees at 'Bob the Baker's' have to wear plastic hats or caps. Why do you think this is?

To stop headlice from jumping into current buns

Jeff has been asked to collect data about the amount of television his friends watch.
Think of an appropriate question he could ask them.

How much TV do you watch?

What guarantees might a mortgage company insist on when buying a house?

They may check to see whether you are well endowed before allowing the purchase.

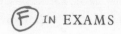

What is a co-operative?

It is a shop which is not as expensive as M&S

What happens during a census?

During the census a man goes from door to door and increases the population.

Assess the major advantages and disadvantages of a greater advancement in scientific knowledge in the twenty-first century.

Too much science to learn at school but at least people didn't die as much.

Suggest the best way for the UK to meet future energy needs.

Drink lots of Lucozade

Discuss the positive and negative aspects of joining a supra-national body such as the UN, NATO or the EU.

everyone hates the EU but the politicians get to go on holiday a lot.

The way people access music has been revolutionised in recent years. Examine what effect this has had on the buying choices of young people.

Lots of people like Susan Boyle now.

Subject: ....**ICT**........

What is a computer virus?

An S.T.D.
A systematically Transmitted Disease.

Joanna works in an office. Her computer is a stand-alone system. What is a stand-alone computer system?

It doesn't come with
a chair

What is hacking?

A really bad cough

The local swimming pool uses a computer system to regulate the water level. Can you suggest a disadvantage of using a computer in this instance?

Computers do not make very good lifeguards.

Can you think of two reasons why Hazel would rather receive an email as opposed to a letter?

1. She doesn't like her postman

2. She hates paper cuts.

Suggest two advantages for shopping online.

1 You don't have to have that horrible "it doesn't fit" moment in the fitting room.

2. You can do it in your pyjamas.

Suggest an advantage to video conferencing.

You can't smell bad breath via video

What is malware?

It is badly made clothing

What is a CD-ROM?

An album of romantic music.

What is a hard disk?

It doesn't break when you put it in the dishwasher.

What is a floppy disk?

It is a disk that has been left
at in the rain

What is a network?

When you chat to people you
don't like to try and get a job.

What is a palmtop?

The leaves of a tropical tree

Give three professions where palmtops are a useful tool.

1. Coconut picker

2. Basket maker

3. Somebody who flaps palm leaves over their boss to cool them down.

What is a desktop?

Where you do your work

What do you use to navigate a desktop?

A map and a compass

Certain storage devices have volatile memory. Briefly explain the meaning of the term 'volatile'.

Like a Vole

List three data validation checks.

1. Ask your mum
2. Ask you brother
3. Wikipedia

Outline one advantage of coding data.

Other people can't read it

Outline one disadvantage of employing graphical user interface.

Costs too much

Applications software is often used for modelling a range of situations. Briefly explain the meaning of the term 'modelling'.

Modelling is when people take pictures of girls with no bras on.

Explain the meaning of the term 'copyright'.

If Someone wants to copy Something Someone else has done, they have to copy it exactly, otherwise it's not copyright.

Subject: **Religious Studies**

What is the significance of an altar?

God knows.!

Christians only have one spouse, what is this called?

Monotony

What do Christians celebrate at Christmas?

When Joseph and Mary had a baby called Jesus. They travelled to Bethlehem by plane and Pontius was their pilot.

What were Jesus' closest group of followers known as?

The 12 decibels

What miracle do Christians celebrate at Easter time?

Chocolate!

Other than Christianity, state two religions.

1 The Force in Star Wars

2 Football

What is the difference between the New Testament and the Old Testament?

The New Testament was a better version.

What is a pilgrimage?

It's when lots of people wander off in the same direction for no apparent reason

Who was Solomon?

He was a very popular man who had 700 wives and 300 porcupines

Suggest how a religious believer might have a meaningful connection to God.

If God adds you as a Facebook friend — that's a meaningful connection.

What is the design argument for God's existence?

The world is designed so crap that
it must have been done by an old man
with rubbish eye sight.

Believing that God is 'transcendent' often helps those
who are suffering. Why is this?

If he was transparent you
couldn't see him.

What is meant by the term 'religious conversion'?

A religious conversion is when a rugby player makes the kick after a try, and some one says 'Jesus Christ, that was a miracle!'

Subject: **Classical Studies**

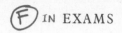

Name one of the early Romans' greatest achievements.

Learning to speak Latin.

Name the successor of the first Roman Emperor.

The second Roman Emperor

Write what you know about Nero.

A really good coffee shop.
Starbucks was his main competitor.

What were the circumstances of Julius Caesar's death?

Suspicious ones

Where was Hadrian's Wall built?

Around Hadrian's garden

What is Spartacus known for?

He was famous for leading a slaves' rebellion in Rome and later he became famous for appearing in a blockbuster movie all about it.

Name the wife of Orpheus, whom he attempted to save from the underworld.

Mrs Orpheus

Who was it that helped Theseus escape from the Labyrinth?

David Bowie

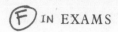

Who wrote *The Republic* and *The Apology*?

Play-doh.

Roman men visited the baths at what time of day?

At Bathtime

2p, or not 2p?

Would you have enjoyed going to school in Sparta?
Give two reasons for your answer.

Yes. Gerard Butler lives in Sparta

How did the Olympic Games originate?

Someone went for a ~~walk~~ run one day
and people watched cos he was naked.

Name one major British road which was originally built by the Romans.

CAESAR STREET

Romans worshipped Gods and divine spirits at home. Name two.

① alcohol
② Asterix

Subject: English

Discuss the style of *Romeo and Juliet*.

It is written entirely in Islamic pentameter. The play is full of heroic couplets, one example being Romeo + Juliet themselves

How does Romeo's character develop throughout the play?

It doesn't, it's just self, self, self, all the way thrash.

How much is Romeo to blame for what happens at the end of *Romeo and Juliet?*

He is completely to blame.
He's an alpha male and
he's named after a car.

Use the word 'judicious' in a sentence to illustrate its meaning.

I am using 'judicious' in this sentence to illustrate it's meaning

Imagine you work for a travel agent. Describe a place you have been to and explain why it would interest someone of a similar age.

My mum and dad drag me to Butlins every year. I wouldn't recommend it to anyone my age.

Why should we be optimistic about the future? Use either a discursive or an argumentative style in composing your answer.

Because if you're not positive about the future then you ain't got much hope have you.

In *Pride and Prejudice*, at what moment does Elizabeth Bennet realise her true feelings for Mr Darcy?

When she sees him coming out of the lake.

Suggest an appropriate word for each of these meanings:

a) An appliance or implement designed to help one do work.

My parents and the Internet

b) To be on water without sinking

Jesus

c) Aggressive; harsh

My brother and my teacher Mrs Topley

d) Faultless or highly-skilled

My answers!

Imagine you are a journalist. Write about the characteristics you think a best friend should have and discuss, giving examples, why you think this.

A Car if they is a boy and nice body if they is a girl.

How is Ralph's character portrayed in Lord of the Flies?

A bit of a sap.
Buzzing around a lot.

Do you dislike any of the characters in To Kill a Mockingbird? If so, why?

I think the mockingbird is shitty. They say in the book that all it does is make music, but for all they know it could be taking the mick in bird language. Why else would they call it a mocking bird?

Pick a celebrity whom you admire and explain why you admire them.

I fancy Robert Pattingson, he is a friendly vampire.

www.summersdale.com